TO - ELSIE MITCHELL —
WHOSE GOLDEN PEGASUS
VOICE COULD SELL ANYTHING
AND FOR HER HELP
GETTING ME STRAIGHT
OUT & PARDON THE
AWFUL
WRITING !
GOOD & LUCK
CHEERS

POTOMAC
WIND
& WISDOM

POTOMAC

Jokes, Lies, and True
Stories By and About
America's Politics
& and Politicians

WIND

& WISDOM

Dick Hyman

ILLUSTRATIONS BY
Marci Davis

The Stephen Greene Press
Brattleboro, Vermont

PUBLISHED JULY 1980
Second printing December 1981

Potomac Wind and Wisdom by Dick Hyman

This book has been produced in the United States of America. It is designed by Douglas Kubach, and published by The Stephen Greene Press.

Library of Congress Cataloging in Publication Data

HYMAN, DICK
  Potomac wind and wisdom.

  Includes index.

  1. United States—Politics and government—Anecdotes, facetiae, satire, etc.   I. Title.
PN6231.P6H94   081   80-13482
ISBN 0-8289-0372-7

Foreword

BY

John Chamberlain

H. L. Mencken's Americana department in the old *American Mercury* may have started it. *The New Yorker,* with its People Who Make News feature, kept it going. But the master of the art of assembling odd, ludicrous and boneheaded items is Dick Hyman.

Less acidulous than Mencken, Dick Hyman is still lots of fun. Who can forget his *Trenton Pickle Ordinance,* an uproarious collection of crackpot enactments dreamed up by the lawmakers of the fifty American states? Earlier there was his *Cock-eyed Americana,* consisting of goof-offs by judges, Rube Goldberg patent seekers, the drawers of wills and the pronouncements of sundry assorted jackasses. Dick's recent *Lest Ill Luck Befall Thee,* an anthology of superstitions, had me laughing in su-

perior fashion, a perhaps unseemly response from one who always tucks a St. Christopher's medal in his pocket before getting into an airplane. It takes Dick Hyman to remind us that we are all human, even in our hypocrisies.

What I like best about *Potomac Wind and Wisdom,* the Hyman latest, is the insight it offers to Presidential character. The star of Hyman's ensemble is none other than Calvin Coolidge, who seldom opened his mouth, but when he did it was always to good purpose. Mencken laughed at Coolidge for making the White House a peaceful dormitory, but during his waking hours "Silent Cal" gave ample evidence of an intelligence that would not have shamed a *Mercury* editor. Once, when Mrs. Coolidge noticed a man on a horse coming toward her in the park, she surmised it must be the willful Senator Borah. "Can't be," said Cal, "the horse and rider are going in the same direction." Could Mencken have put it better?

Abraham Lincoln's humor was genial and general: It was not ordinarily designed to hurt, though in dealing with the procrastinating General McClellan, Abe sometimes forgot himself. Lincoln was never an enemy of action. Going to a

funeral in a slow-moving wagon, he wondered whether the horse would get the corpse to the grave in time for the Resurrection.

Teddy Roosevelt's humor was of a more savage kind, and it depended chiefly on adjectival vigor. Those who criticized T.R. on Panama were "a small body of shrill eunuchs." William Howard Taft—"Big Bill"—relished stories at his own expense. He particularly liked the child at the beach who said, "We won't be able to go in today; the President is using the ocean." Woodrow Wilson, believe it or not, did have humor before the turmoil of his second term engulfed him. Could it have been that he forgot his own observation, "Every man who takes office in Washington either grows or swells"?

Franklin Roosevelt's humor was subtly patronizing; Harry Truman's was direct ("If you can't stand the heat, get out of the kitchen"); Lyndon Johnson's was elemental; Hoover's was rueful; Jack Kennedy's had an elegant edge. Hyman's selections constitute good portraiture. The reader learns while laughing.

It is not only in the White House that Dick Hyman has planted his tapes. He has eavesdropped

at the Gridiron Club, he has haunted the halls of Congress, he has gone on the hustings. It's all grist for Dick in *Potomac Wind and Wisdom*—and the surprising fact, considering he is dealing with politicians, is that there is more wisdom than wind. Could it be that there is hope for the Republic in that?

ACKNOWLEDGMENTS

Most of the jokes and stories in POTOMAC WIND AND WISDOM were collected by the author during a lifetime of listening to and telling jokes about America's politics and politicians. Others were gathered from particular sources, including those noted in the text, and also including the following. To these humorists, writers, and publishers, the author and publisher are grateful (and so is the reader—or he should be!): Harold Brayman, *The President Speaks Off the Record* (Dow Jones Books, 1976); George Fuermann in the Houston *Post* (quoted in *Reader's Digest*, "Laughter, the Best Medicine"); James C. Humes, *Speaker's Treasury of Anecdotes about the Famous* (Harper & Row) (quoted in *Reader's Digest*, "Laughter"); Richard Ketchum, *Will Rogers: The Man and His Times* (American Heritage, 1973); John H. McKee, *Coolidge Wit and Wisdom* (New York: Stokes, 1933); Bob Orben, *Orben's Current Comedy* (quoted in *Reader's Digest*, "Laughter"); Winston Pendleton, *Two Thousand One Hundred Twenty-One Funny Stories and How to Tell Them* (St. Louis: Bethany, 1964).

POTOMAC
WIND
& WISDOM

Politician Defined

A politician is a guy who shakes your hand before an election and your confidence afterwards.

Simon Cameron, American politician: "An honest politician is one who, when he is bought, will stay bought."

The Best and the Brightest

Representative Davidson Henderson, Democrat of North Carolina, tells one about a man who returned to his native town after twenty years' absence and asked his uncle about a former friend.

"Well, Tom tried farming for awhile but went broke," he responded. "Then he went to law school, but he failed to make a living as a lawyer."

"That's too bad," said the nephew. "Everybody liked Tom. I'm sorry to hear he's such a failure."

"Failure?" cried the uncle. "He's our Congressman!"

4

The Oldest Profession

A surgeon, an engineer, and a politician were disputing: which of their occupations was the oldest? The doctor insisted that the first profession was surgery, because Eve was created by carving a rib out of Adam. The engineer held that his profession was older still, for before the creation of Adam and Eve there had to have been Earth created from chaos—an engineer's job.

"All right," the politician finally said, "but who do you think made the chaos?"

A Clear Explanation

Adlai Stevenson told of a little boy who heard his father talking about converts and traitors and said to him, "Father, what is the difference between a convert and a traitor?"

The father replied, "Well, son, don't you understand—if a Republican becomes a Democrat, he is a convert, but if a Democrat becomes a Republican, he is a traitor."

A Game of Strategy

Somebody once observed that politics is a game of strategy: the people try to figure out what the politician stands for, and the politician tries to figure out what the people will stand for.

FDR's Definitions

Franklin D. Roosevelt had an elegant wit, which he exercised in puns and, especially, in humorous definitions (or *were* they strictly humorous?). Among FDR's definitions: "A Conservative is a man with two perfectly good legs who has never learned to walk; a Radical is a man with both feet planted firmly in the air; and a Reactionary is a somnambulist walking backward."

The Effects of Office

Woodrow Wilson had a reputation for quiet wit. It was Wilson who said, "A Conservative is a man who just sits and thinks, mostly sits."

Another Wilson saying, to be taken to heart by every would-be holder of national office: "Every man who comes to Washington either grows or swells."

Goodbye, Morrissey

One of the jovial guests at a dinner for Kennedy aide Ken O'Donnell was Michael DiSalle, former Democratic Governor of Ohio. In the storytelling spirit of the evening, he offered this one:

"Two men were walking together one Sunday afternoon. One said: 'Did you hear that Morrissey joined the Republican party?' The other replied: 'I don't believe it. I saw him in church only this morning.'"

The Carter Wit

President Jimmy Carter's humor is dry, quick, and sometimes biting. At one point the President was asked at a press conference for a reaction to the Kremlin's expulsion of an Associated Press reporter from the Soviet Union. It was a time of strained relations between the Carter White House and certain members of the press; and President Carter began his answer by wondering if the Kremlin's act entitled the White House to expel an AP correspondent, too.

9

Thank You, Friend

Every politician has his favorite story about do-good citizens who show up with kind words and offers to help after elections are won, not before.

Representative Dan Kuykendal, Republican of Tennessee, has the topper.

A man walked up to Kuykendal on a Memphis street after his successful campaign, slapped him on the back, pumped his hand vigorously and said sincerely:

"If I'd know'd you was going to win, I'd of voted for you."

Another morning-after story concerns Calvin Coolidge.

The diffident Coolidge was little known even to his neighbors in Northampton, Massachusetts. Not all of them appreciated Cal's total self-possession. One day shortly after Coolidge's election as Mayor of Northampton, early in his career, one of his neighbors met him on the street and spoke up.

"I didn't vote for you," he told the new Mayor.
"Somebody did," Cal said, passing on.

Statesman Defined

T. B. Reed, powerful Senator from Maine early
in this century, had the classic definition:

"A Statesman is a politician who is dead," said
Boss Reed.

Silent Cal

There are probably more kinds of stories about Coolidge's wit and humor than there are about any other President—which is curious, for Coolidge almost never said or did anything at all. His taciturn and thrifty type of Yankee humor, with its unobtrusive irony, was so low-keyed that no one has ever been able to figure out whether Silent Cal was very simple or very deep.

One famous Coolidge story that illustrates Cal's verbal economy relates the time Mr. Coolidge went to church alone one Sunday. When he returned, Mrs. Coolidge said, "How was the sermon?"

"Fine," replied Mr. Coolidge.

"What did the minister talk about?" asked the First Lady.

"Sin," said the President.

"What did he have to say about it?"

"He was against it," twanged Mr. Coolidge.

At one point during the Coolidge presidency, the animated and gracious Mrs. Coolidge sat for a White House portrait by the painter Howard

Chandler Christy. The First Lady wore a red velvet evening dress, and was posed with a favorite dog. Her dress seemed a little too blatant to the President. Christy, however, wanted the bright splash of color in the portrait. "Why not," Coolidge proposed, deadpan, "paint her in a white dress, and paint the dog red?"

Another story of the Coolidge wit has it that a woman came up to the President after a speech he had given in a crowded hall. "I enjoyed your speech so much that I stood up the whole time," the lady told him.

"So did I," said Cal.

Cal Counts the House

This Coolidge story occurred on the campaign trail. His train made a stop at a small town. Coolidge walked out onto the rear platform and looked at the sparse gathering.

He stood there for a moment, then turned and walked back into his private car.

Inside he explained, "This crowd is too big for an anecdote and too small for an oration."

Coolidge and the Banker

The story is told of Calvin Coolidge that after he became Vice President in 1920 he was flooded with offers to become an honorary member, officer, or trustee in many organizations. One such offer came from a recently opened Washington bank. The bank's president called on Coolidge to solicit a small deposit. "Even a few dollars would be a great honor," the banker insisted.

"Why don't you make me an honorary depositor?" Vice President Coolidge suggested.

A Short Conversation

Maybe the most famous Coolidge story of all is set at a fancy Society dinner party thrown by a celebrated Washington hostess—the kind of affair

President Coolidge detested. Go he must. The President was seated beside his vivacious hostess, who determined to put his renowned silence to the test for the amusement of her other guests.

"Oh, President Coolidge," she bubbled, "I've made a bet with the others that I can make you say three words tonight. What do you say to that?"

"You lose," the President said.

Slow Down!

The late Senator Hubert Humphrey was the polar opposite of the laconic Calvin Coolidge. Humphrey loved to talk, and he talked a lot—at high speed.

Senator Barry Goldwater once took note of this. At the time, Humphrey was serving as Lyndon Johnson's Vice President.

"As you know, the Vice President speaks kind of fast," Goldwater said. "I was listening to one of his recent talks when a reporter sitting next to me

muttered: 'Trying to get anything out of this speech is like trying to get something out of *Playboy* magazine with your wife turning the pages.' "

A Matter of Apportionment

A Congressman, campaigning for re-election, was working a crowd when one voter, apparently not impressed with his record, shouted, "Hey, I wouldn't vote for you if you were Saint Peter himself!"

"If I were Saint Peter," the candidate came back, "you *couldn't* vote for me: you wouldn't be in my district."

A Heckler Humiliated

Politicians are forever speechifying, debating, declaiming; and some of the best political stories tell of orators and their sometimes uncooperative audiences.

20

While campaigning in Ohio, President William Howard Taft's speech was interrupted when one of the more vocal dissidents tossed a ripe cabbage onto the platform.

Taft paused for a moment and with perfect timing said, "I see that one of my opponents has lost his head."

TR Takes One on the Chin

President Theodore Roosevelt, facing a packed audience, was interrupted by a man who had had a few too many and objected loudly to Teddy's remarks. Finally he shouted to the Republican standard bearer, "I am a Democrat!"

Teddy asked the man why and the man replied, "Because my father was a Democrat; my grandfather was a Democrat and so I'm a Democrat."

Teddy quieted the crowd with: "Let me ask you this, sir. If your father was a jackass, and your grandfather was a jackass, what would you be?"

"A Republican," said the drunk.

Tell 'Em All You Know

Once, when Al Smith had paused in a speech because a heckler kept interrupting him, the man shouted, "Go ahead, Al, don't let me bother you. Tell 'em all you know. It won't take you long."

Smith, always quick on the trigger, replied: "If I tell 'em all we both know it won't take me any longer."

When it came to political insult, Al really had the gift. Of his arch-opponent, Col. Theodore Roosevelt, Jr., he complained, "If bunk were electricity, the Colonel would be a powerhouse!"

Stop!

"Fellow citizens," shouted the political candidate, "I have represented you at the capital at a great sacrifice to myself. I have neglected my home and family. I have fought, I have strived, I

have———." "Stop, you've done enough for us," came a voice from the crowd. "We'll vote for your opponent!"

Oompah! Oompah!

President Harry Truman told this story about himself. It happened during the 1948 campaign on an Indian reservation. He spoke of what he would do for the Indians if he was returned to office. At the conclusion of each of his promises, the crowd shouted, "Oompah! Oompah!"

Inspired by this show of support, Truman went on with new vigor about an improved life for the Indians if he got back to Washington.

"Oompah! Oompah!" came the response.

At the end of his speech he started back to his train and had to cross a big corral which had been packed with horses. Treading lightly and carefully, Truman's Indian guide said to him, "Careful, don't step in the Oompah!"

A Voice from the Rear

In today's world of sophisticated electronic equipment, it's hard for a speechmaker to go unheard—barring of course, a power failure.

But things go wrong in the best of loudspeaker systems, and the results can be disastrous sometimes.

When his mike suddenly went dead in the middle of a speech, a Congressman continued on lung power alone for a few sentences then paused to ask:

"Can everyone hear me?"

"I can't hear a word you're saying," bellowed a voice from the back of the hall.

"I can hear him perfectly," shouted someone in the front row. "Want to trade places?"

The Facts Are These . . .

Whenever he gets one of those ultra-lavish introductions at a speech, Representative George Grider, Democrat of Tennessee, says:

"Thank you for that overly generous introduction. I hate to deny its accuracy, but it does remind me of the time a speaker was introduced as a man 'who had made a million dollars in oil in California.'

"This man pointed out politely that it wasn't California, but Pennsylvania, and that it was coal, not oil. Also, he said, it wasn't a million dollars, just half a million. Then he observed that it was his brother, not him.

"And finally, he pointed out, his brother didn't make it. He lost it."

Powerful Interests

During an election, two candidates for the office of Mayor in a small Southern town were engaged in a knock-down, drag-out debate.

Finally one candidate jumped to his feet, leveled a finger at the other, and challenged: "I dare you, sir, to tell me about the powerful interest that controls you!"

"Now wait a minute," roared the accused. "You leave my wife out of this!"

You Had to Ask, Woodrow

President Woodrow Wilson, a fan of Mark Twain, stopped off at Hannibal, Missouri, Twain's birthplace.

He wandered around and saw a native lounging idly by.

"Is this where Tom Sawyer was supposed to have lived?"

The native looked at Wilson, "Who?"

"Tom Sawyer," Wilson replied.

"Never heard of him."

"How about Huckleberry Finn?" asked the President.

"Nope," said the native, "don't know him either."

"Well," said the President, "how about Pudd'n-head Wilson?"

☆☆☆☆☆☆☆☆☆☆☆☆☆☆☆☆☆☆☆☆☆☆

30

"Oh," said the native, "sure, why I even voted for him."

In another famous Wilson story, the President was awakened at 4 A.M. by a call from an eager young man who informed him that the commissioner of highways had just died.

"I know he'll be a hard man to replace, Mr. President," the caller said, "but I thought I would be a good man to take his place."

"It certainly is all right by me," answered Wilson, "if it is all right by the undertaker."

Fred from Jones County

A Senator was in his home state to give an address to the state committee of his party. After his speech the Senator and the committee officers formed a receiving line to greet the party rank and file. One member of the audience, when he reached the Senator in the receiving line, said, "That speech of yours was absolutely the worst

I've ever heard." Not wanting to hold up the receiving line—especially for an embarrassing scene—the Senator gave the fellow a big smile, shook his hand, and moved him along to the next person in the line. Not long afterward, however, the same man came through the line again. This time he said, on reaching the Senator, "Your ideas were all tired, stupid and unworkable." Again the Senator moved the man along, smiling. But to his horror the man came back a third time, and again lambasted the beleaguered solon: "Judging by that speech you're an insult to the party and the whole state." The Senator, sweating now, could only move his assailant along once more. He saw with relief that the affair was breaking up.

After the guests had left the Senator was talking to one of the committeemen who had been in the receiving line with him. He asked the man who the fellow was who had come through the line three times, each time launching a more bitter attack on the Senator and his speech.

"That's Fred from Jones County," the committeeman said.

"He really gave me hell," the Senator remarked.

"Oh, don't take Fred too seriously," the other laughed. "He only says what he hears from everybody else."

Miseries of Defeat

Following his first defeat by Eisenhower, Adlai Stevenson had this to say at a dinner:

"It is now some three months, nine days, nineteen hours, and forty-seven minutes since we conceded the election to General Eisenhower. In that interval, General Eisenhower has had the honors of victory and also the misery, while I have had the miseries of defeat and also a vacation. But, as the newspapers say, to the victor belongs the toil."

Stevenson's Fate

Stevenson was famous for his understated humor. In addressing the American Society of Newspaper Editors in Washington one time, Stevenson,

☆☆☆☆☆☆☆☆☆☆☆☆☆☆☆☆☆☆☆☆☆☆

who lost to General Eisenhower in two successive Presidential elections, apologized for arriving late. He had been held up at the airport by the simultaneous arrival of President De Gaulle of France. Stevenson said: "It seems my fate to be always getting in the way of national heroes."

Benefits of Age

On Herbert Hoover's eightieth birthday, which he celebrated at his birthplace, West Branch, Iowa, he was asked if he still had any bitterness about the way he was cruelly pilloried during and even after his White House years.

"No," Hoover said. "I have no hatred for anybody, any more. But your question reminds me of the story of an old fellow about my time of life who attended a prayer meeting at which the preacher spoke of brotherly love. When the preacher asked if there was anyone in the congregation who could honestly say he did not have a single enemy, this old fellow stood up and said, 'Right here, parson. I don't have one enemy.'

35

"The preacher commended him on the exemplary life he must have led, and then asked him to explain how he had come to be so universally beloved that he hadn't a single enemy.

" 'I outlived the bastards!' the old party shouted."

Defeat Is Bitter

Representative G. V. (Sonny) Montgomery, Democrat of Mississippi, tells a story to illustrate how tough things can be in violent Neshoba County. It's about a political candidate who ran and got licked and then put this ad in a local paper:

"I lost several weeks canvassing. I lost several acres of corn and potatoes. I gave away 2 calves and 5 goats for barbecue.

"I gave away 5 pairs of suspenders, 6 ladies' dresses and 15 baby rattles. For prospective voters I plowed 173 acres and spread 63 loads of barnyard fertilizer. I drew 25 buckets of water, put up

14 kitchen stoves, kindled 17 fires and kissed 115 babies.

"I walked 6,481 miles, shook 9,847 hands, talked enough to make several volumes. I lost 2 front teeth and some hair in a personal encounter with a supporter of my opponent. I attended 26 revival meetings, made love to 9 grass widows, and got dog bit 39 times and *folks, I still got defeated.*

"I want to thank my 43 *friends*—and they are my friends—for casting their votes for me; and the rest of Neshoba County, I warn you that I am now going armed with a sawed-off shotgun, because a man who doesn't have any more than 43 friends in a county as big as Neshoba is definitely in need of protection."

"If You Lived Here . . ."

At a 1968 dinner, then-Representative Gerald R. Ford told how he loved the House of Representatives, but said that sometimes late at night on his way home, as he went past 1600 Pennsylvania

Avenue, he seemed to hear a little voice saying, "If you lived here, you'd be home now."

Candidate Exposure

Lyndon Baines Johnson had a vein of broad, Texas-style humor. He delighted in applying down-home stories to Washington situations. Once LBJ remarked,

"I see by the papers that Goldwater and Rockefeller have decided to cut down on their appearances in California. This reminded me of the fellow in Texas who said to his friend, 'Earl, I am thinking of running for sheriff against Uncle Jim Wilson, what do you think?' 'Well,' said his friend, 'it depends on which one of you sees the most people.' 'That is what I figure,' said his friend. 'Sure,' Earl went on, 'if you see the most, Uncle Jim will win. If he sees the most, you will win.' "

Bound for Glory?

One of LBJ's favorite stories from his Texas hill country concerned a man who always slept through the sermons at church. "Every Sunday," according to the President, "he'd come and get in the front row and sleep all during the sermon. Finally, the preacher got a little irritated, and one Sunday he said, 'All you people who want to go to Heaven, please rise!' Everyone stood up except this one man, who was sound asleep, as usual. When the people sat down, the preacher said in a very loud voice, calculated to arouse the sleeper, 'Now, all of you who want to go to Hell, please stand up!' The man jumped up. He looked around him, in back of him, he looked at his wife, and she was sitting down, at his children, and they were sitting down. He looked at the preacher, somewhat frustrated, and said, 'Preacher, I don't know what it is we are voting on, but you and I seem to be the only two who are for it.' "

Before a number of Democrats at a dinner, LBJ said, "Talking to Democrats about the qualities of our party, and the shortcomings of the opposition,

is like the preacher telling the people who are already in their pews what a sin it is not to come to church."

Small Parties

Said by President Johnson: "I think that it is very important that we have a two-party country. I am a fellow who likes small parties and the Republican Party is about the size I like."

Air Force One

Lyndon was known as a President who took advantage of the perquisites of his high office.

Idaho Governor Robert Smylie, Representative George Hansen and some other Idahoans hooked a ride with President Johnson when he winged westward on Air Force One for one of his "nonpolitical" tours.

The Idaho group looked forward to the trip

eagerly, having heard that life aboard Air Force One is fairly luxurious. Said one of the President's guests:

"I understand you get a Purple Heart if you get hit with a champagne cork."

The Eternal Revenue Service

One of President Johnson's special stories concerning money is about a letter written by a little girl which reached the Postmaster General. It read:

"Dear God: Please send Mom $100 to help with the family."

The Postmaster General was so touched by the plaintive plea that he took a twenty dollar bill from his pocket and forwarded it to the little girl. A few days later another letter from the same girl arrived at his office. It read:

"Dear God: Please send $100 for Mom. But this time don't send it through Washington. The tax people deduct 80 per cent."

The Farm Bill

Another favorite story of LBJ's concerned one of his eager young aides:

"Not long ago I called in one of the very bright and very busy young men I have working with me, and I said to him—rather brusquely because I was in a hurry: 'The people want to know what we are going to do about the Farm Bill. Let's get our recommendations up right away.' He came right back and said: "Mr. President, I don't think we have to consider that. I don't have a file on any Farm Bill. I will look it up, but I think you ought to go tell them that if we owe it, we will pay it."

LBJ and the Press

President Johnson made a list of his tormentors and his champions among the Washington correspondents and columnists.

"I've got thirty-one biased against me and four biased in favor of me," he said.

Ouch!

President Johnson was making a serious statement about crime in the country, and thus wasn't playing the barb game.

He got one, anyway, off a newspaper headline. The headline read: "LBJ Says Crime Second Biggest U.S. Headache."

"That Lyndon!" said a GOP wit on Capitol Hill, "he always wants to be first."

A Fish Story

Former California Governor Ronald Reagan, campaigning for the Republican Presidential nomination in 1976, told this story apropos the politician's tendency to make empty promises.

"A shipload of canned fish was interned in an Italian port, during the last war, and when finally released for sale, the cargo brought $25,000. It was then resold for $50,000, and, as the war years went on, that shipment of canned fish kept changing hands until, finally, it brought $600,000.

"The last purchaser opened a can and tried the fish. Enraged, he got on the phone and demanded that something be done because the fish was spoiled. And he was told by the man who sold it to him, 'But that fish isn't for eating; it's for selling!'"

Promises, Promises

An old story has it that there used to be a first aid course for Congressmen, Senators and others in government. At one session of the course the instructor asked a Congressman what he'd do if he came on a person in a faint.

"I'd give him a shot of whiskey," said the Congressman.

"What if you didn't have any whiskey," the instructor asked.

"I'd promise him some," the Congressman answered.

The politicians who were promising two cars in every garage last year are now busily engaged putting up new parking meters.

DeLuxe Breadlines

A politician was making a speech in the heart of the slum area. "When I'm elected," he thundered, "you won't see that long, dreary breadline. When I'm elected, there'll be two breadlines—one for white and one for rye!"

Give 'Em Hell, Harry!

President Harry S Truman explained his "Give 'em hell" speeches this way:

"I never give them hell," he said, "I just tell the truth, and they think it is hell."

The Longworth Retort

Nicholas Longworth of Ohio, son-in-law of Theodore Roosevelt, and Speaker of the House of Representatives in the Twenties, is credited with one of Washington's most famous put-downs. The

Speaker's baldness was often the butt of jokes from his political opponents. On one occasion one of these, a Congressman, playfully passed his hand over Longworth's bald pate and impudently commented, "Feels just like my wife's bottom."

Longworth then passed his own hand over his head, and remarked, thoughtfully, "You know, it does, doesn't it?"

In School?

When freshman Democratic Representative Lester Wolff of New York defeated conservative Republican Steven Derounian in November, 1964, a key campaign issue was school prayer.

Derounian, a staunch defender of the right to pray in school, once bellowed during a speech:

"The right to pray is as sacred as the mother's right to nurse a child."

From the back of the room, a thin female voice queried:

"In school?"

School Prayer

Former Senator Sam Ervin of North Carolina told a famous story about a Carolina school teacher around the time the Supreme Court banned prayer in public schools.

This teacher went into her classroom about fifteen minutes before the class was supposed to begin work and caught a bunch of her boys down in a huddle on their knees in the corner of the room. She demanded of them what they were doing, and one of them hollered back and said, "We're shooting craps." She said, "That's all right, I was afraid you were praying."

The Chaplain's Prayer

Not all prayer that affects politicians takes place (or doesn't take place) in schools.

Edward Everett Hale (1822–1909), Chaplain of the United States Senate, was asked, "Dr. Hale, when you look at the state of our country and the world, do you pray for the Senators in your charge?"

"No," the venerable clergyman answered. "When I look at the Senators I pray for our country."

The Second Office

A lot of wit has been aimed at Vice Presidents, Lieutenant-This-and-That's, and other governmental second bananas. Alben Barkley, Truman's Vice President, put the matter this way:

"Two brothers were born to a family in Kentucky. When they grew up one ran off to sea, the other became Vice President of the United States. Neither one was ever heard from again."

Calvin Coolidge apparently shared Barkley's views of second-office holding. In one Coolidge story, Cal was at a dinner during his tenure as Lieutenant Governor of Massachusetts. A lady at the same dinner asked him what he did.

"I'm the Lieutenant Governor," he told her.

"My," said the lady, "that must be interesting. Tell me about it."

"I just did," said Cal.

Cheer for Convention Alternates

Will Rogers once said: "Now a delegate is bad enough, but an alternate is just a spare tire for a delegate. An alternate is the lowest form of political life there is. He is the parachute on a plane that never leaves the ground."

Ex-Presidents

President Harry Truman told a newsman upon retiring from office, "All Ex-Presidents do is take pills and dedicate libraries."

No Landslide

The Kennedy family is known for its great wealth, gathered by patriarch Joseph Kennedy in his many enterprises. The Kennedys' political opponents have tried to turn the family's wealth against them. Never successfully, however, for the Kennedys have had the good sense to turn the advantages of wealth into a subject for self-deprecating humor. A celebrated instance was during the Presidential campaign of John F. Kennedy in 1960. At one gathering, before starting his speech, Jack Kennedy reached into his pocket and took out a piece of paper, which, he announced, was a telegram from his father. "Dear Jack," he pretended to read, "don't buy a single vote more than is necessary. I'm damned if I'll pay for a landslide."

The Reluctant Hero

JFK was even capable of turning his distinguished record as a PT boat commander in World

55

War II to humorous purposes. Asked how he became a war hero, Kennedy answered, "It was involuntary. They sank my boat."

A Warm Hand

An opening line that got John Kennedy off right at a Los Angeles rally was:

"I appreciate your welcome. As the cow said to the Maine farmer, 'Thank you for a warm hand on a cold morning.' "

Career Counseling

Barry Goldwater, an amateur photographer, took a snapshot of President Kennedy and sent the photo to the President for an autograph.

Kennedy inscribed the picture thusly: "For Barry Goldwater, whom I urge to follow the career for which he has shown so much talent—photography. From his friend, John Kennedy."

☆☆☆☆☆☆☆☆☆☆☆☆☆☆☆☆☆☆☆☆

☆☆☆☆☆☆☆☆☆☆☆☆☆☆☆☆☆☆☆☆☆☆

When Jefferson Dined Alone

In 1962 President Kennedy invited forty-nine American winners of the Nobel Prize to dinner at the White House. It was one of the great cultural occasions in recent American history, and it was also the occasion for a famous display of the Kennedy wit. Addressing his illustrious guests, the President said, "I think this is the most extraordi-

nary collection of talent, of human knowledge, that has been gathered together at the White House—with the possible exception of when Thomas Jefferson dined alone."

On-the-Job Training

John F. Kennedy, after his election as President, was a speaker at a dinner. He had been criticized for appointing his younger brother, Robert F. Kennedy, as Attorney General. The President wryly suggested at that dinner that he had good reasons for the appointment.

"Bobby wants to practice law, and I thought he ought to get a little experience first."

Goldberg Gives

John F. Kennedy, at an annual convention of the AFL–CIO referred to the then Secretary of Labor Arthur Goldberg in his speech. He said: "Goldberg had been lost on a mountain-climbing expedition in Switzerland.

"They sent out search parties and there was no sign that afternoon or night. The next day, the Red Cross went out and around, calling 'Goldberg, Goldberg, it's the Red Cross!' Then the voice came down the mountain, 'I gave at the office!' "

JFK's Rocker Explained

A great comment made about President Kennedy's much publicized rocking chair came

from Senator Everett Dirksen, who said, "It gives you a sense of motion, with a sense of danger."

Affairs of State

Alben Barkley, Vice President under Harry Truman, was a great story teller. Here is one of his best.

Said Barkley: "When I was in the House, I was told that the difference between the House Foreign Affairs Committee and the Senate Foreign Relations Committee was that the Senators were too old to have affairs. They only have relations."

Off the Record

Alben Barkley was in excellent form while sitting as President of the Senate when the Senator from Tennessee complained that the Senator from Illinois was yawning at him.

The Vice President said without cracking a smile: "The yawn of the Senator from Illinois will be stricken from the record."

"What Jines Mine"

Abraham Lincoln is the first President to be famous for his wit, which was rustic and subtle at the same time.

In a debate in Congress on the war with Mexico, he recalled the Illinois farmer who declared: "I ain't greedy about land. I only want what jines mine."

The One-Holer

There is a famous Lincoln story, set in the course of the Civil War, about a visit of the President to the field headquarters of General George McClellan, who was known to be an indecisive commander. Lincoln and his aide called on the General at his tent, but found no one there. Hearing hammering from the woods nearby, they went to see if McClellan was there. They came to a group of soldiers at work building a small structure. Lincoln asked what it was.

"A privy for the General," answered one of the soldiers.

Lincoln was silent for a moment, then asked, "Is it a one-holer or a two-holer?"

"A one-holer," came the answer. Lincoln seemed satisfied.

Lincoln's aide was puzzled by the President's question; but as the two walked away, Lincoln remarked, "Thank God it is a one-holer, for if it were a two-holer McClellan would beshit himself before he could make up his mind which hole he should use."

How to Write a Nasty Letter

An aide of Lincoln's once became angry at someone who had maltreated him about his actions on a political matter. He asked Lincoln for advice. Lincoln told him to write a letter explaining the matter and letting the offender know exactly how it feels to be victimized like that.

"Tell him everything that bothers you," said

Abe, "and in no uncertain terms."

"Should I mail it or have it delivered by messenger?" asked the lad.

"Neither—rip it up when you finish. You'll feel much better."

Blame the Speechwriter

When Kenneth Keating was a Senator from New York, he was said to have once made a classic remark. He said: "Roosevelt proved a man could be President for life; Truman proved anybody could be President; and Eisenhower proved you don't need to have a President." He later denied it and blamed it on his speechwriter.

The Speechwriter's Revenge

Speechwriters take a lot of blame from the politicians who employ them. Sometimes they strike

☆☆☆☆☆☆☆☆☆☆☆☆☆☆☆☆☆☆☆

back. In one such case, a Senator had called his head writer on the carpet, bawled him out for not doing his job, and fired him. That evening the Senator was delivering an address to an audience of influential business and community leaders. Speaking from his prepared text, he had hit his stride, and he had his audience's rapt attention. "Our country, our economy, must cast off the twin toils of inflation and unemployment," the Senator intoned. "We can do this, and at a single

stroke! There is one measure which we in Congress can take that will relieve our besetting woes. The measure is—"

The Senator had reached the end of the page of his text. He turned the page. To his horror he found the sheet beneath it empty except for one line:

Now you're on your own, you son of a bitch.

An Invitation with a Meaning

George Dixon, one-time famous columnist whose "Washington Scene" appeared in many newspapers from coast to coast, wrote:

"The recurrence of a name in the Washington social pages frequently hints that the owner of the name is about to be lifted into prominence. If I'd only read between the menu lines of our food-maddened society writers, I think I could have foretold that a local lawyer named Dean Acheson would become Secretary of State. One hostess ac-

tually did put two and two together in this case, but she wasn't sure enough of her arithmetic to go all the way. She compromised by phoning the august Mr. Acheson. 'A little bird tells me,' she cooed, 'that the dear President is about to name you Secretary of State. If it goes through will you please come to dinner Friday night? If it doesn't, come in afterward for dancing.' "

The Cave that Ran for President

John F. Parker, a State Senator in Massachusetts, compiled a book of political campaign jokes and anecdotes entitled *If Elected, I Promise,* which includes the one about the party boss who stopped at a rural gas station in Maine to sound out local opinion about the race for Governorship.

"I don't know much about it," said the elderly proprietor of the service station, "but if stickers on the bumpers of automobiles mean anything, the candidate to watch is this fellow Ausable Chasm."

Equal Opportunity in Democracy

Clarence Darrow, the most celebrated lawyer of his time, made the conclusive remark on the thesis that in America high political power is within the reach of all. Surveying the political scene, Darrow mused, "When I was a boy I was told that anyone could become President. I'm beginning to believe it."

Take a Stand!

A candidate for the United States Senate had finished a speech before a tough audience. The question-and-answer period had begun. The Press was there in force, the speech was important, and the candidate was being very careful not to take a position that would offend any interest.

"What's your view on Foreign Aid?" came a question.

"I'm right on that issue, too," the politician replied, deadpan.

Our political leaders, it seems, have not always been eager to reveal the passionately held convictions that have compelled them to the public service.

Back in 1892, the Vice Presidential candidate, Adlai E. Stevenson, grandfather of the former United Nations delegate, was making a railroad whistle stop tour of the Northwest where the paramount issue of the campaign was whether the mountain peak which dominates the landscape should be called Tacoma or Rainier. At some stops the citizens were pro-Rainier . . . at other stops, pro-Tacoma. It was impossible to avoid the issue. With the aid of the engineer, Stevenson arranged a showmanly device. In every speech he made reference to the beauty of the mountain and referred to the controversy over its name.

"This controversy," he said, "must be settled and settled right by the national government. I pledge myself, here and now, that if elected I will not rest until this glorious mountain is properly named. There is only one appellation which is worthy of consideration, and that is ———." Here he pulled the cord which the engineer had installed, whereupon his voice was instantly

drowned by the scream of the engine whistle, whereupon the train pulled out of the station. The sentence was never completed and nobody ever figured out where Stevenson stood on the Tacoma–Rainier controversy.

President Lyndon Johnson told a story about a Texas schoolteacher that is appropriate to the subject of politicians who waffle their positions. The teacher had applied for a post in a country school, and was being examined by the school board. An examiner asked him, "Do you believe the world is flat or round?"

"Doesn't matter," the teacher replied. "I can teach it either way."

Sage Advice

In his book *Year of Decision* former President Harry Truman writes: "During one of my first sessions in the Senate, J. Hamilton Lewis came over and sat down by me. He was from Illinois and was

the Whip of the Senate at that time. 'Don't start out with an inferiority complex,' he told me. 'For the first six months you'll wonder how you got here—and after that you'll wonder how the rest of us got here.' "

You Can Lose Your Burro

A famous Ronald Reagan story about the pitfalls of political waffling concerned a man who was going down the road one day with his son, leading a burro. They met another man, who said to them, "Don't you realize you shouldn't both be walking on this hot day? You have that burro. One of you at least should be riding."

So the father thought this was a good idea, and put his son on the burro and continued to lead the burro until they met a second man. The second man said, "Don't you realize the burro is a beast of burden, perfectly capable of carrying both of you. There is no reason why either one of you should walk."

And they both got on and rode, until they met

a third man, who said, "How can you do that on a hot day like this? How can you be so cruel to a poor dumb animal? The two of you should be carrying the burro."

So the father and son tied the burro's feet together, swung him over a pole, put it on their shoulders, and went down the road. Presently they came to a bridge. When they started across the bridge with this unaccustomed and concentrated load, the bridge collapsed and they were plunged into the torrent below. Well, they both managed to make it to shore, but the burro, with his feet tied together, drowned.

And the moral is . . . you can lose your burro trying to please everyone.

The Company He Keeps

When Republican Senate leader Everett Dirksen announced that a new "grass roots" movement was under way in support of his constitutional amendment to modify "one man-one vote" reapportionment, Sen. Frank Church, Idaho Democrat,

was sitting with him. Church, generally classified as a liberal, seemed just a bit discomfited in company with his conservative colleague. Asked later how he felt about supporting a measure sponsored by Dirksen and so many other conservatives, Church defined his reaction by telling this story.

"A school teacher asked all those in her class of youngsters to raise their hands if they wanted to go to heaven. All but one shot their hands up.

"The kid who didn't raise his hand was kept after class a moment. The teacher asked him, 'Johnny, why didn't you raise your hand with the others? Don't you want to go to heaven?'

"Johnny replied: 'Sure I do, but not with this crowd.' "

Our Greatest President

William Howard Taft, President from 1909–1913, was the greatest man who ever held the office in one very real sense. Taft weighed three hundred pounds in his socks. As President, he required a custom-made outsize bathtub to be in-

stalled in the White House. A genial, very intelligent, and progressive leader, Taft was perhaps the only American President who thoroughly relished stories at his own expense. Early in his Presidency, he went with his party to a wedding in New England. His aide, Major Archie Butt, wrapped in gold braid, was the focus of all eyes. A conversation between the hostess and her Irish gardener after the ceremony was repeated by Taft. "Ah, it was a foine occasion," said the gardener.

"Yes, and wasn't it pleasant to have the President of the United States?" the hostess added.

"Yes, madam, yes it was," responded the gardener. "He's a foine looking man and what a beautiful uniform he had. But who the devil was the fat old man that was following him around?"

Taft at the Beach

One of the stories Taft told was about his vacation trip to a New England beach. Walking toward the ocean for a dip in the surf, he was spotted by several children also going in for a dip.

Spotting Taft, one of the youngsters held the others back.

"We won't be able to go in today," he said, "the President is using the ocean."

Jokes and Laws

Will Rogers was America's greatest political humorist, and one of its greatest humorists in any subject. It was said he could make even President Cal Coolidge laugh—once. Somebody once asked Will, who was forever roasting politicians, what was the difference between a Congressman and other public figures, like himself. Will reflected a moment, then said, "Congressmen and fellows like me are alike in some ways, I guess. But when I make a joke, it's a joke. When *they* make a joke, it's a law."

Then Will reflected some more, and added, "And when they make a law, it's a joke."

Another time, Will Rogers mused to his audi-

ence, "You know, Congress is a strange place. A man gets up to speak and says nothing, nobody listens, and then everybody disagrees."

"Congress Deadlocked!"

Will Rogers once remarked that the Washington papers were headlining, "Congress Is Deadlocked and Cannot Act."

"I think this is the greatest blessing that could befall this country," said Will.

Another Will Rogers observation was that Election Day and Hallowe'en come near falling in the same week. These two holidays are of equal importance, Will said, but folks seem to have more fun on Election Day than on Hallowe'en. "On Hallowe'en they put pumpkins on their heads and on election they don't have to."

Meet Your Senator

Will Rogers once suggested in his newspaper column that somebody start a Meet Your Senator Week, the idea springing from Will's observation that members of that body are seldom if ever to be seen in their home states except immediately before elections. In another column a few weeks later, Will wrote: "You would be surprised at the amount of resentment that has come to my roll

top desk . . ." as a result of his Meet Your Senator idea. "That's why they elected him," Will wrote, "it was to get rid of him. If they had wanted him at home, they would have kept him at home."

A Farmer at Heart

A delegation from Kansas, calling upon Theodore Roosevelt at Oyster Bay, was met by the President with coat and collar off. "Ah, gentlemen," he said, mopping his brow, "I'm delighted to see you, but I'm very busy putting in my hay just now. Come down to the barn and we'll talk things over while I work."

When they reached the barn there was no hay waiting to be thrown into the mow. "James," shouted the President to his hired man in the loft, "where's the hay?"

"I'm sorry sir," admitted James, "but I just ain't had time to throw it back since you forked it up for yesterday's delegation."

The Rough Rider

During the Spanish American War Teddy
Roosevelt organized the Rough Riders, a melange
of cowboys, ex-polo players, and ex-convicts. He
always considered a former Rough Rider better
qualified for any appointment than any other as-
pirant, although he was aware of weaknesses in
this theory. In 1906, when Secretary of War Taft
(a graduate of Yale), asked for the nomination of

another Yale man to some post in the Southwest, President Roosevelt ruefully acquiesced: "I guess Yale '78 has the call, as there seems to be no Rough Rider available, and every individual in the Southern District of the Indian Territory (including every Rough Rider) appears to be either under indictment, convicted, or in a position that renders it imperatively necessary that he *should be* indicted. Let us therefore appoint George Walker, Yale '78, charge to Taft, and see if the Senate (God bless them!) will confirm him."

Homecoming

A traveler on an airplane struck up a conversation with the passenger seated beside him. The first admitted to the other that he was uneasy. "I was just released from prison," he said, "and I'm on my way back home. It'll be tough facing old friends."

"I know just how you feel," the other said. "I'm on my way home from Congress."

☆☆☆☆☆☆☆☆☆☆☆☆☆☆☆☆☆☆

Nixon and the Big Contributor

When John F. Kennedy was campaigning for the Presidency in 1960 he told a story on then-Vice President Richard Nixon, his opponent. Nixon was said to disapprove strongly of profanity, especially in the language of public figures. Kennedy said Nixon was perfectly truthful in claiming to disapprove of profanity; but he went on to recount a conversation supposed to have occurred between Nixon and a wealthy Republican. The Republican was complimenting the Vice President on a speech he had just finished.

"Best damned speech I ever heard," he said.

"I appreciate the sentiment, but not the language," candidate Nixon replied.

The Republican then continued, "Yes, I thought so much of that speech that I've decided to contribute five thousand dollars to your campaign."

"The hell you say," Nixon said.

(Maybe he really said something like, "expletive deleted" . . .)

☆☆☆☆☆☆☆☆☆☆☆☆☆☆☆☆☆☆☆☆☆

Think about This One

Comedian Mort Sahl had the best of the bumper crop of Watergate jokes that were making the rounds a couple of years ago. He claimed that the entire blame for the Watergate Affair and the constitutional crisis it precipitated really fell on George McGovern, the Democratic candidate for President in 1972 against Richard Nixon. Yes, surprising as it may seem, Watergate really was all McGovern's fault. For, Sahl concluded, "If Nixon had been allowed to run unopposed, he would have lost."

"I Do Not Choose to Run"

California Governor Pat Brown was talked about as a potential Presidential contender in 1960. In an interview, he declared that in order that there be no question of any availability he would like to declare courageously and unequivo-

cally, that "I am not a candidate for President in 1960."

"If this doesn't put me in the thick of the race, I don't know what will," Brown observed.

Baby-Kissing

In the heat of campaigning, candidates will often step out of character to make the voter-pleasing gesture. Not Senator Barry Goldwater of Arizona, however, who claims to eschew such theatrics.

"I've never been a bagel eater or steel cap wearer or baby kisser," Barry avers. "I think a man ought to be natural. If the baby's twenty-one, I'll think about it."

Grappling with the Issues

Robert Bendiner, newspaper columnist, on the 1952 Presidential campaign: "One top Republican has coined the phrase 'Fear Deal' and another

proposes the war cry: 'Pink, Mink and Stink.'
Naturally, we can't expect the campaign to stay
on this high a plane when the going really gets
tough."

The Log Cabin

Ever since the mid-1800's it has been common
for American political candidates to claim hum-
ble birth. The number of our presidents allegedly

born in log cabins, for instance, defies the laws of probability. Opposing candidates often vie with each other for poorest childhood. One Indiana politician is supposed to have topped his opponent in crying poor by admitting he wasn't born in a log cabin, but then going on to recall that his family moved into one as soon as they could afford it.

The Celibate Extrovert

Another story of Massachusetts State Senator John F. Parker concerns the famous speech that Senator George Smathers of Florida is alleged to have given in the illiterate back country of Florida in 1950, ruining his opponent, Claude Pepper:

"Are you good folks aware that Senator Pepper is known all over Washington as a shameless extrovert? Not only that, but this man practices nepotism with his sister-in-law, and he has a sister who was once a thespian in wicked New York

City. Worst of all, before his marriage, Claude
Pepper habitually practiced celibacy."

On the Junket

Comic Bob Orben, a bemused observer of the
political scene, reflects, "Our Congressman just
came back from a fact-finding trip to Las Vegas,
Honolulu, Paris and Monte Carlo.

"Boy, those facts sure know where to hide."

Door-to-Door

Representative Glenn R. Davis, Republican of
Wisconsin, was campaigning door-to-door, and at
one home was greeted by a little girl. Davis introduced himself, explained his business and asked
the tot if she'd summon her mommy.

"I'm sorry," the little girl said, upon returning.
"My mommy said to tell you she's asleep."

Combat Pay

Gerald Ford is an ardent golfer, and one who, as President, had few illusions about the quality of his game. Discussing his proneness to drive the ball into the spectators' gallery during his golf matches, President Ford once remarked that when he was on the links his Secret Service escort got combat pay.

Qualified for the Job

Leonard Lyons, former syndicated newspaper columnist, said:

"One of my favorite political jokes involved ex-Governor Michael V. DiSalle of Ohio. When he was elected Mayor of Toledo, he was asked by a man he had known for years to name him to the job of City Treasurer. DiSalle reminded him: 'But you know nothing about arithmetic. I doubt even that you can add.' To which the man replied: 'That's right, Mike. But I am not asking for the

job of Assistant Treasurer or Deputy. I am asking for the job of City Treasurer.' "

What, Four?

The late Adam Clayton Powell, Congressman from New York City, was famous for his junkets, which were seldom solitary. Journalist Fletcher Knebel once cracked, "Clayton Powell may soon be off to Europe again with his female secretaries. When reporters asked him What for, Powell said 'No, five.' "

Ethnic Solidarity

Many stories swell the fat file of David Powers, famed "court jester" to the late John Kennedy.

One sample from Powers:

At a precinct caucus there were two candidates for leader—Sullivan and Swenson. Voting were

107 Irishmen and 3 Swedes. When the votes were cast, Sullivan got 107 and Swenson 3.

A little later Sullivan commented to a friend: "Say those Swedes are a clannish lot, aren't they?"

Strong Leadership

Apropos of certain New Deal farm proposals, former President Herbert Hoover paid his respects to "politicians who live by the sweat of the farmer's brow.

"The administration may not know where they are going," Hoover said, "but they are taking us with them."

Republican Issues

The acid Fletcher Knebel, addressing Washington's Gridiron Club in the Election Year 1964, remarked that "Republican Chairman Miller says his party has more issues this year than

it knows what to do with. That's not news. It has been years since the Republicans had an issue they knew what to do with."

On the same occasion, Knebel took aim at Senator Barry Goldwater, who was then running for President. In his primary campaigns, Goldwater had been getting the name of an extremist because of certain of his quoted statements. "Senator Goldwater confesses that he made some campaign mistakes in New Hampshire," Knebel observed. "He shouldn't blame himself, though. A man can't always get laryngitis when he needs it."

"Not in the House"

Walter Belson, lecturer and retired public relations executive, has some remarks on Washington humor:

"One of the classic jokes about life in Washington goes something like this:

"A Congressman is awakened in the middle of

the night by his wife who whispers, 'I think there's a burglar in the house.'

" 'Not in the House,' her husband says. 'Perhaps in the Senate, my dear, but not in the House.' "

Personal Ingratitude

Fiorello La Guardia, one time Mayor of New York City, said in scorn for the "bosses" after he became Mayor: "My first qualification for this

great office is my monumental personal ingratitude."

Another La Guardia story tells of Fiorello's humiliating one of his department heads by roaring at a secretary, "If you were any dumber, I'd make you a Commissioner."

Grassroots Support

A political candidate was canvassing for votes in a rural district. His young son accompanied him. Together they would drive from house to house and talk to the voters. On the basis of the reception they received, the candidate's son would scratch out the names of voters who were against his father's candidacy; and in this way the candidate had a measure of the support he could expect in the region.

At one point the candidate and his son pulled up before an isolated farmhouse, parked, and got out of the car. As they were walking up the path

to the house they saw a shotgun pointed at them out the window, and heard an enraged voice shouting at them. "I know who you are, you miserable, low-down parasite! You baby-robber, grafter, filthy crook! Get to hell off my property before I blow you to Kingdom Come!" With that the farmer fired a blast from his shotgun that went just above their heads. The candidate and his son fled back to their car and sped away. Driving along the road, the boy got out his voter tally sheet and asked his father, "Guess I'd better scratch him out, huh, Dad?"

"Certainly not," the candidate replied. "Just put him down as doubtful."

An Urgent Matter

There is a story about a Congressional candidate in Texas who got an urgent call from the manager of his campaign in Houston. "Jim, you'd better get over here right away," the manager said. "The opposition is telling a lot of lies about you around the city."

"Can't come today," the candidate told him. "I've got to go to Dallas."

"But, Jim, this is important. They are telling lies about you in Houston," the manager protested.

"Dallas is even more important," said Jim. "They're telling the truth about me there."

Politics No Threat

Finally, from Will Rogers once again, we close with this thought: "Every time we have an election, we get in worse men and the country keeps right on going. Times have proven only one thing and that is you can't ruin this country, ever, with politics."

INDEX